TWO PIANOS, FOUR HANDS – INTERMEDIATE LEVEL

COMPOSER SHOWCASE
HAL LEONARD
STUDENT PIANO LIBRARY

Piano Concerto No. 2 in G Major

FOR TWO PIANOS, FOUR HANDS

BY MATTHEW EDWARDS

To access audio visit:
www.halleonard.com/mylibrary

Enter Code
4572-3774-7522-7029

ISBN 978-1-4234-1607-4

HAL•LEONARD®

7777 W. BLUEMOUND RD. P.O. BOX 13819 MILWAUKEE, WI 53213

In Australia Contact:
Hal Leonard Australia Pty. Ltd.
4 Lentara Court
Cheltenham, Victoria, 3192 Australia
Email: ausadmin@halleonard.com.au

Visit Hal Leonard Online at
www.halleonard.com

Commissioned by the Greater Laurel Maryland Music Teachers Association

Piano Concerto No. 2 in G Major

for Derek Galvin

I

Matthew Edwards
Op. 7

 simile

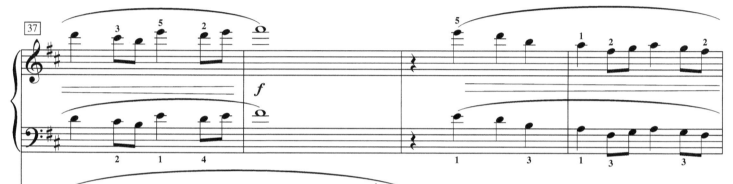

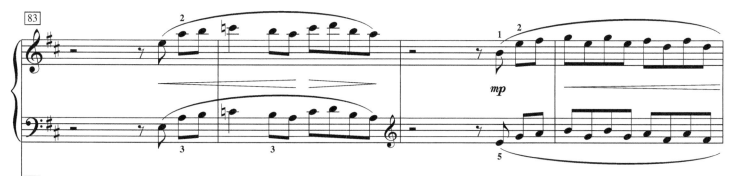

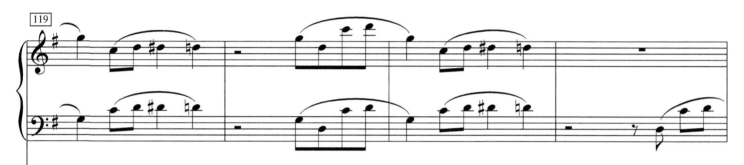

II

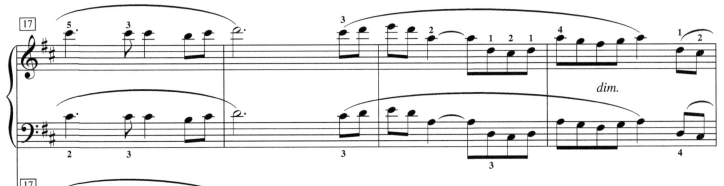

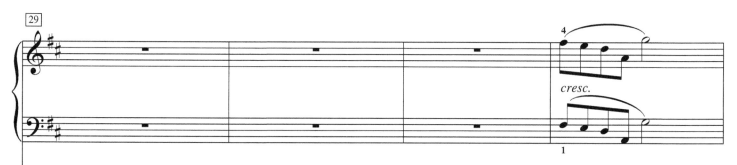

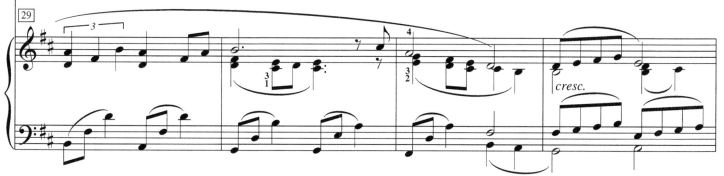

COMPOSER SHOWCASE
HAL LEONARD
STUDENT PIANO LIBRARY

NATIONAL FEDERATION
Junior
Festivals
Choice
2008-2010
OF MUSIC CLUBS

TWO PIANOS, FOUR HANDS – INTERMEDIATE LEVEL

Piano Concerto No. 2 in G Major

FOR TWO PIANOS, FOUR HANDS

BY MATTHEW EDWARDS

In Three Movements:

Maestoso

Andante

Allegro animato

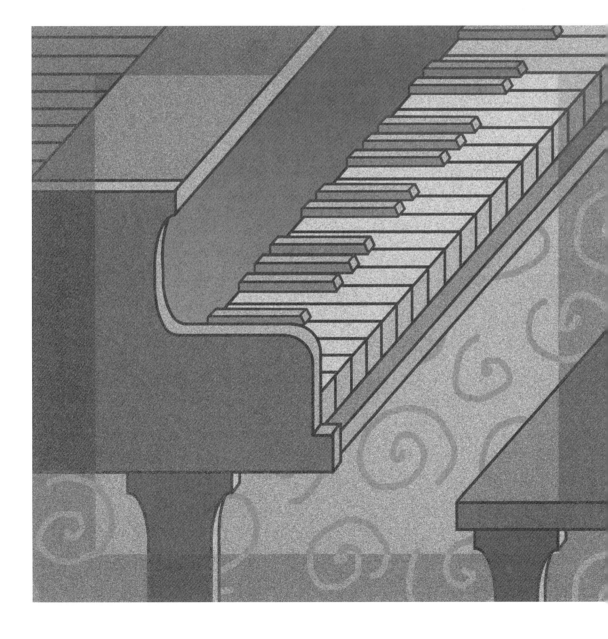

HAL•LEONARD®
7777 W. BLUEMOUND RD. P.O. BOX 13819 MILWAUKEE, WI 53213

HL00296670

Piano Concerto No. 2 in G Major

for Derek Galvin

I

Matthew Edwards
Op. 7

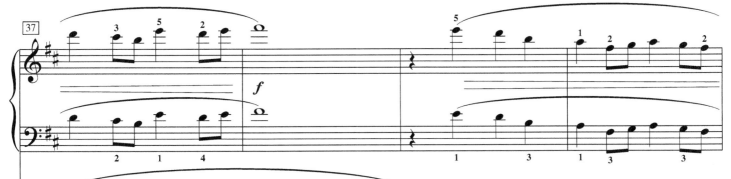

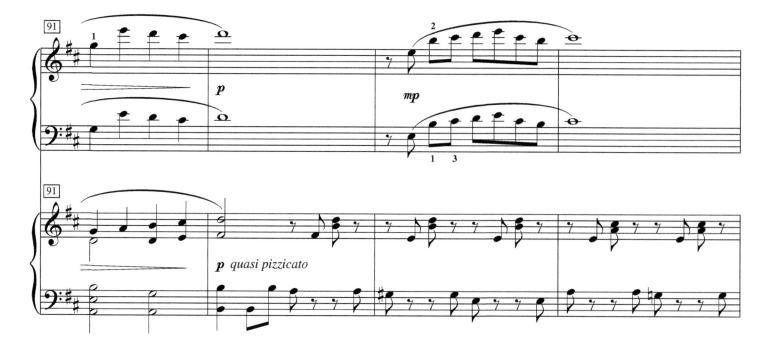

11

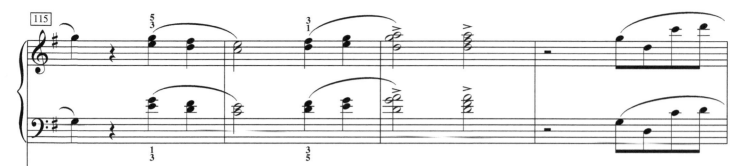

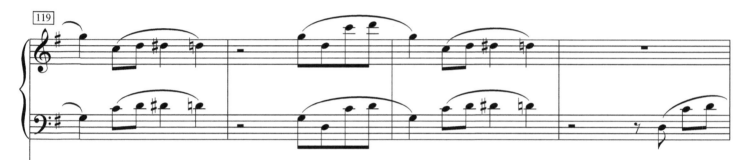

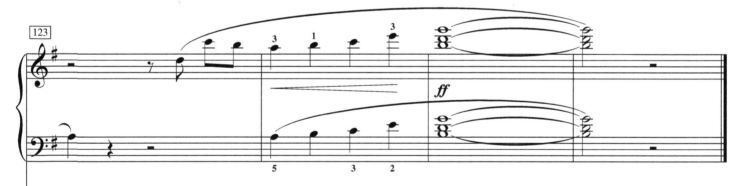

II

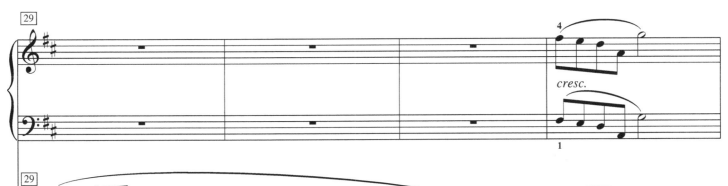

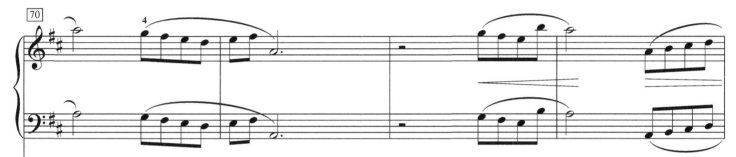

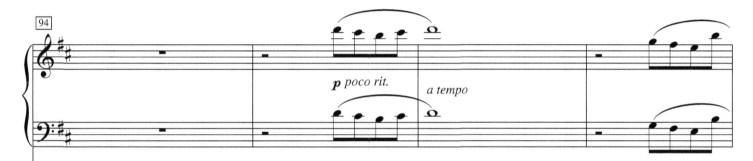

III

22

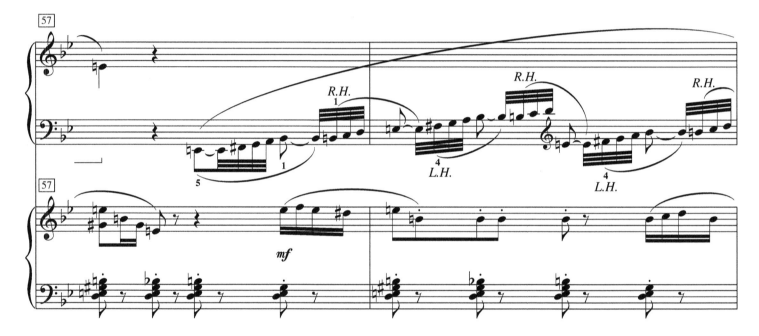

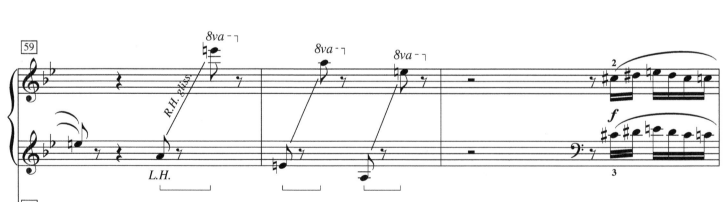

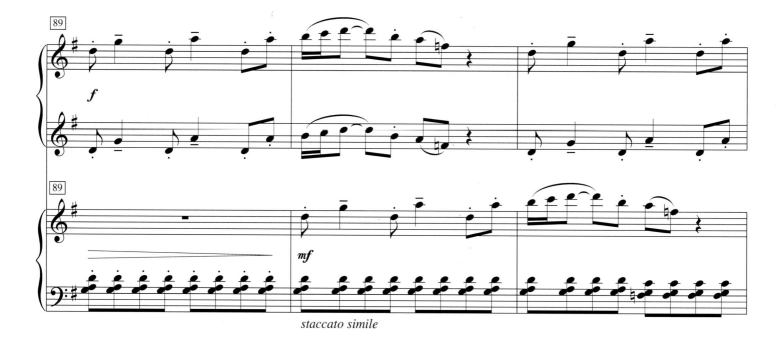

staccato simile

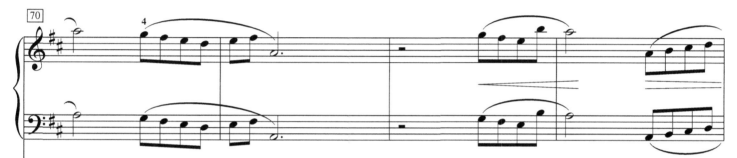

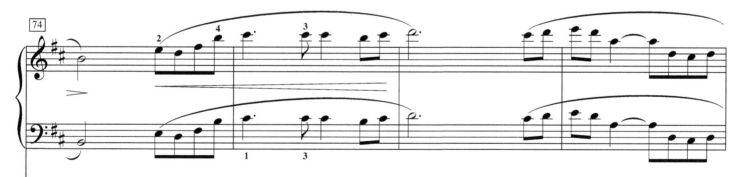

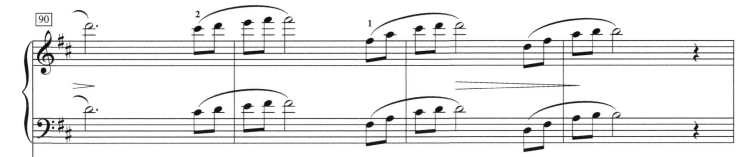

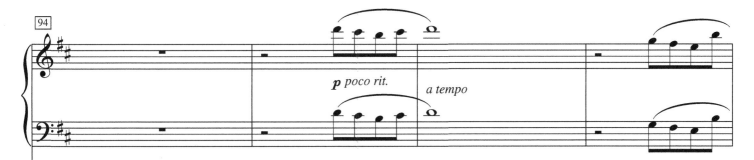

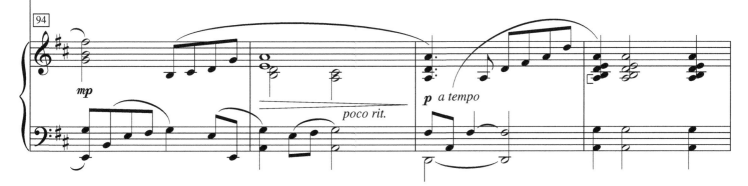

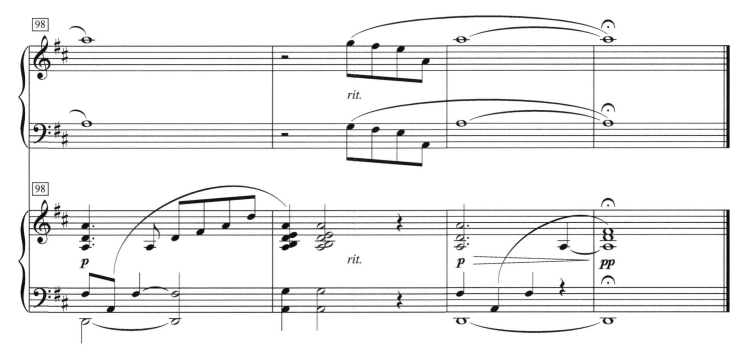

III

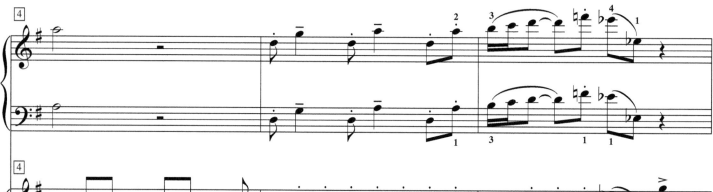

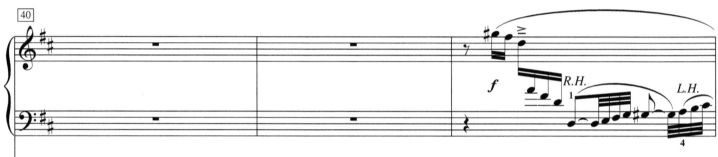

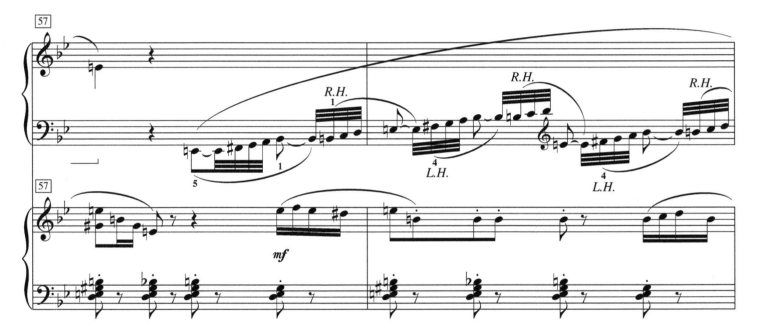

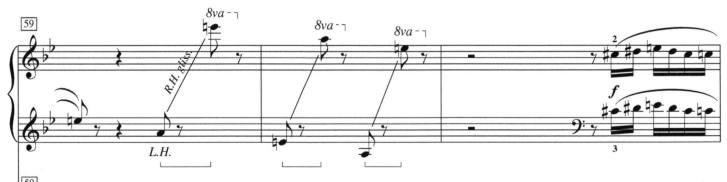

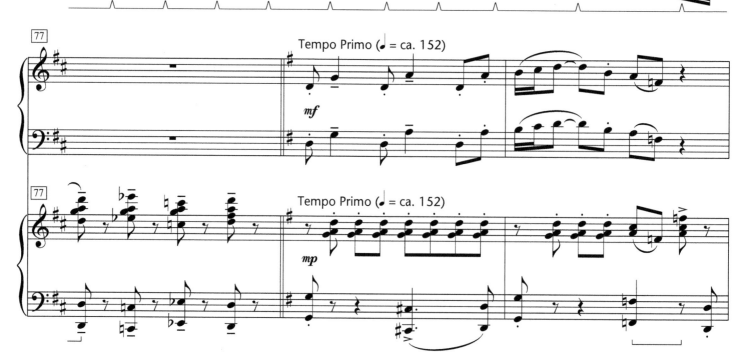

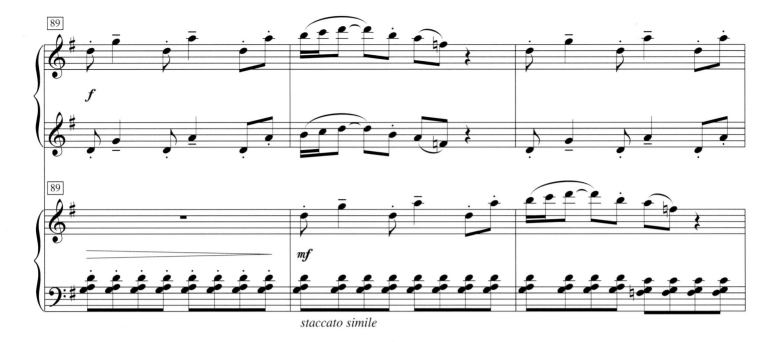

staccato simile

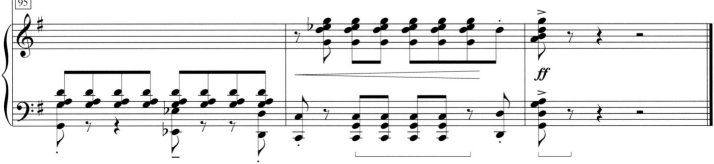